VIOLIN
82VN

S0-BKN-676

THE ARTIST'S STUDIO FOR STRINGS

BOWING DEVELOPMENT STUDIES

by Frank Spinosa & Harold W. Rusch

ISBN 0-8497-3242-5

© 1989 Neil A. Kjos Music Company, 4382 Jutland Drive, San Diego, CA. International copyright secured. All rights reserved.
Printed in U.S.A.
WARNING! The text, photographs and music in this book are protected by copyright law. To copy or reproduce them by any method is an infringement of the copyright law. Anyone who reproduces copyrighted matter is subject to substantial penalties and assessments for each infringement.

The Authors

Frank Spinosa is internationally recognized as a violin soloist, conductor, chamber musician and violin pedagogue. During past summers he has been artist-in-residence at International String Festivals where he has performed with the New Art String Quartet and has conducted International String Festival Orchestras. He has been advisor to the University of Illinois String Research Project directed by Paul Rolland and has served numerous times as Headmaster for the University of Illinois String Summer Youth Division.

As violin soloist, Dr. Spinosa has appeared with the Phoenix Symphony and with other orchestras in the United States. In addition to his position as 1st violinist in the New Art String Quartet, he is currently professor of Music at Arizona State University.

A native of Wisconsin, **Harold Rusch,** is noted around the world as composer, music educator and clinician. After his graduation from Lawrence University in Appleton, Wisconsin, Mr. Rusch started a lifelong career in music which began with teaching.

For over 25 years, Mr. Rusch taught in the Wisconsin Public Schools. During his teaching career he also spent much of his time composing music for school orchestras and bands. Due to the wide acceptance of his compositions, he quit teaching and worked full-time writing methods and concert pieces.

Mr. Rusch continues to actively participate in the musical growth of the country as writer and consultant. He is also represented in the *International Who's Who of Musicians.*

TABLE OF CONTENTS

FOREWORD 6

UNIT ONE 8

Natural Hand Position
The hand position is placed with slight spaces between the first and second fingers and between the third and fourth fingers. Contact point with the bow is closer to the first crease of the index finger.

Controlled Spiccato in the lower third of the bow 8

UNIT TWO 12

Natural Hand Position
The hand position is placed with slight spaces between the first and second fingers and between the third and fourth fingers. Contact point with the bow is closer to the second crease of the index finger.

Controlled Spiccato in the middle third of the bow 12
Sautillé in the middle third of the bow 17
Tremolo in the middle third and upper third of the bow 21
Ricochet in the middle third and upper third of the bow 25
Arpeggiando Saltando in the middle third of the bow 29
Up Bow Flying Spiccato and Jeté in the middle third of the bow 33

UNIT THREE 38

Extended Hand Position
The hand position is placed with larger spaces between the first and second fingers and between the third and fourth fingers with the second and third fingers placed slightly deeper. Contact point with the bow is closer to the first crease of the index finger.

Collé in the lower third and the upper two thirds of the bow 38
Ruvido (rough) Détaché in the lower third of the bow 42
Chordal Playing in the lower third of the bow 45
Portato (Louré) in the upper two thirds and the lower third of
the bow 47

UNIT FOUR 52
Extended Hand Position
    The hand position is placed with larger spaces between the first
    and second fingers and between the third and fourth fingers
    with the second and third fingers placed slightly deeper. Contact
    point with the bow is closer to the second crease of the index
    finger.
Martelé in the upper two thirds and lower third of the bow 52
Fast Up Bow Staccato in the upper two thirds and lower third of the bow ...55
Slow Staccato in the upper two thirds and lower third of the bow 59
Smooth Détaché in the upper two thirds and lower third of the bow 63
Accented Détaché (Serré) in the lower third, middle third and upper third
of the bow 67
Expressive Détaché (Détaché Chanté or Détaché Porté) in the lower
third, middle third and upper third of the bow 72
Fouetté Détaché (Whipped Détaché) in the middle third of the bow 75
Lancé Détaché (Speared Détaché) in the upper third of the bow 78
Sustained Whole Bow Stroke (Son Filé) 82
Legato String Crossings 85
Détaché String Crossings in the middle third of the bow 89

UNIT FIVE 94

Additional Bowing Articulations
Bariolage 94
Mixed Bowings—Recovery-Type Bowing Patterns 97
Mixed Bowings-Alternation-Type Bowing Patterns 102

UNIT SIX 105

General Pedagogical Considerations

INDEX OF BOWINGS 108

INDEX OF COMPOSERS AND COMPOSITIONS 109

Foreword

An essential tool to string playing is the bow. Having control of the bow and properly executing the infinite styles and varieties of bow articulations is an ongoing challenge for players at all levels of advancement. Proper implementation of bow articulations begins with the setting of the fingers of the right hand. There is **not** one fixed position but rather, slight variations in the bow hold effecting specific articulations with more natural results. The following pages illustrate through photos, exercises, etudes and classical literature, four basic settings, how they are executed and the articulations which the settings produce naturally.

The following terms will be used throughout this book and are considered necessary in implementing the four basic settings for the right hand:

CENTER OF BALANCE—The 'ring' formed by the right thumb and the first crease of the second finger in the bow hold. This serves as a focal point for the four basic settings of the right hand.

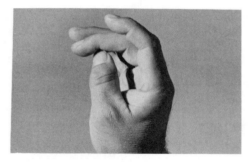

The center of balance between the thumb and middle finger. The thumb is curved.

The thumb supports the bow at the frog near the upper right corner of the thumb nail.

STRING LEVEL—The proper height for the right elbow in relation to the string(s) being played. Let the right elbow naturally follow the placement of the index finger, palm outward, across the particular string(s) to be played.

String Level: E String

String Level: G String

SUPINATION—The clockwise rotation of the right forearm and upper arm so as to lean toward the third and fourth fingers. The wrist is in its natural position.

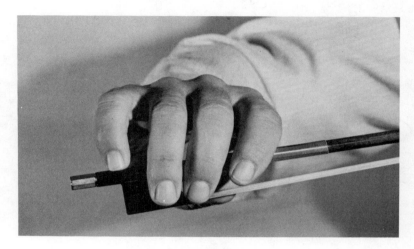

Supination

PRONATION—The counterclockwise rotation of the right forearm and upper arm so as to lean toward the first (index) finger. The wrist is slightly indented.

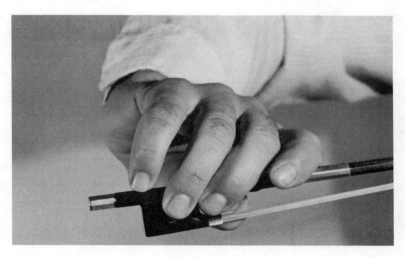

Pronation

The CENTER OF BALANCE and STRING LEVELS must be established as initial steps for each bowing articulation.

UNIT ONE
Natural Hand Position

I. Description
    A. slight spaces between the first and second fingers and between the third and fourth fingers
    B. contact point with the bow is closer to the first crease of the index finger

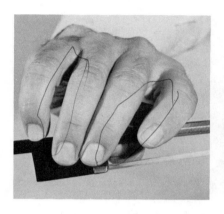 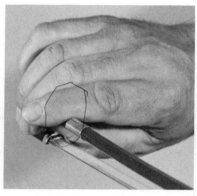 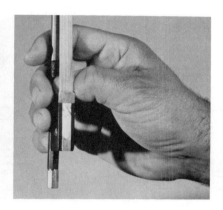

II. Ideal bowings
    A. controlled spiccato in the <u>lower third</u> of the bow

III. Pedagogical tips (for practice examples)
    A. supinate the forearm
    B. flatten the bow hair
    C. initiate silent vertical bowing motions on all indicated pitches, maintaining a relaxed posture in the upper arm, forearm and hand
    D. after mastering proper rhythm and string levels, add a slight lateral motion to the bowing strokes, accenting the up bow*
    E. after mastering examples 1 and 2, apply solutions to Mazas Etude No. 25 and the excerpt from the first movement of the Violin Concerto in D Major, Op. 35 by Peter I. Tchaikovsky

EXAMPLE 1

Controlled spiccato — lower third of bow
Jacques Fereol Mazas, No. 25
open string practice
meas. 1–8

*The up bow requires a slight accent since it works against the natural gravity of the body.

ETUDE

Jacques Fereol Mazas, No. 25

EXAMPLE 2

Controlled spiccato — lower third of the bow
P.I. Tchaikovsky
Violin Concerto in D Major, Op. 35 (1st Mvt.)
open string practice
meas. 111–113

VIOLIN CONCERTO IN D MAJOR
1st Movement — Excerpts

Peter I. Tchaikovsky, Op. 35

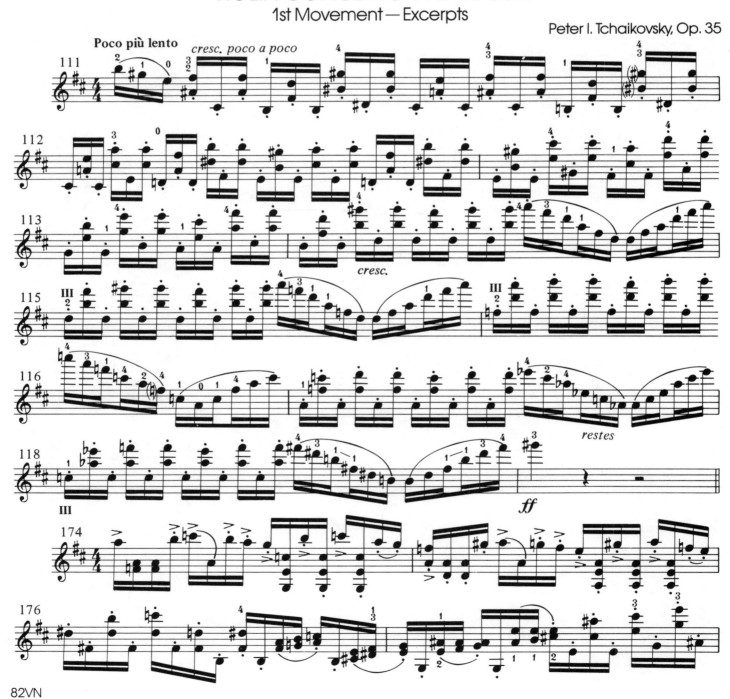

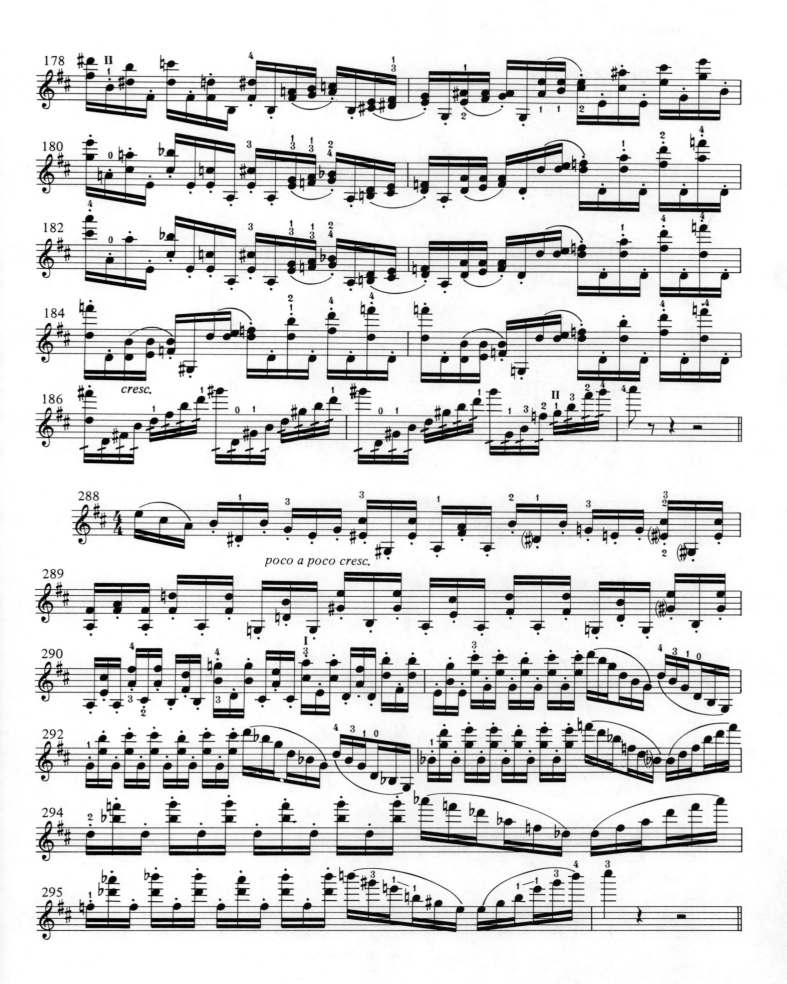

UNIT TWO
Natural Hand Position

I. Description
    A. slight spaces between the first and second fingers and between the third and fourth fingers
    B. contact point with the bow is closer to the second crease of the index finger

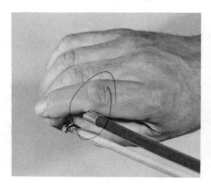 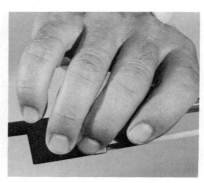 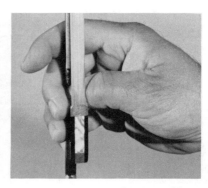

II. Ideal bowings
    A. controlled spiccato in the middle third of the bow
    B. sautillé in the middle third of the bow
    C. tremolo in the middle third and upper third of the bow
    D. ricochet in the middle third and upper third of the bow
    E. arpeggiando saltando in the middle third of the bow
    F. up bow flying spiccato and the jeté in the middle third of the bow

III. Pedagogical tips for **controlled spiccato** in the <u>middle third</u> of the bow
    A. supinate the forearm
    B. flatten the bow hair
    C. initiate silent vertical bowing motions on all indicated pitches, maintaining a relaxed posture in the upper arm, forearm and hand
    D. after mastering proper rhythm and string levels, add a slight lateral motion to the bowing strokes, accenting up bow
    E. after mastering examples 3 and 4, apply solutions to Rode Etude No. 17 and the Scherzo movement from String Quartet in C Minor, Op. 18, No. 4 by Ludwig van Beethoven

EXAMPLE 3

Controlled Spiccato — middle third of bow
Pierre Rode, No. 17
open string practice
meas. 1–15

ETUDE

Pierre Rode, No. 17

14

82VN

EXAMPLE 4

Ludwig van Beethoven – String Quartet, Op. 18, No. 4 (Scherzo)
open string practice
meas. 10–26

STRING QUARTET IN C MINOR
2nd Movement — 1st Violin Part

Ludwig van Beethoven,
Op. 18, No. 4

16

82VN

IV. Pedagogical tips for sautillé in the middle third of the bow
  A. supinate the forearm for a lighter sautillé sound and pronate
     slightly for a heavier grittier sautillé sound
  B. flatten the bow hair
  C. initiate a rapid tremolo type bowing motion at the tip of the bow
     and move slowly toward the middle of the bow
  D. the right hand motion should be in a direction that is diagonal to
     the shaft of the bow
  E. at a particular point in the bow the wood will begin to bounce
     against the hair, while the hair maintains contact with the string*
  F. after mastering examples 5 and 6, apply the solutions to Kreutzer
     Etude No. 9 and the Piú Allegro section of the Introduction and
     Rondo Capriccioso, Op. 28 by Camille Saint-Saëns

EXAMPLE 5

Sautillé — middle third of bow
Rodolphe Kruetzer, No. 9
open string practice
meas. 1–9

*If the speed of the stroke is reduced the bounce will occur closer to the frog. If the speed of the stroke
is increased the bounce will occur closer to the tip.

ETUDE

Rodolphe Kreutzer, No. 9

EXAMPLE 6

Sautillé — middle third of bow
Camille Saint-Saëns
Introduction and Rondo Capriccioso, Op. 28
open string practice
meas. 309-315

INTRODUCTION AND RONDO CAPRICCIOSO
Excerpt

Camille Saint-Saëns, Op. 28

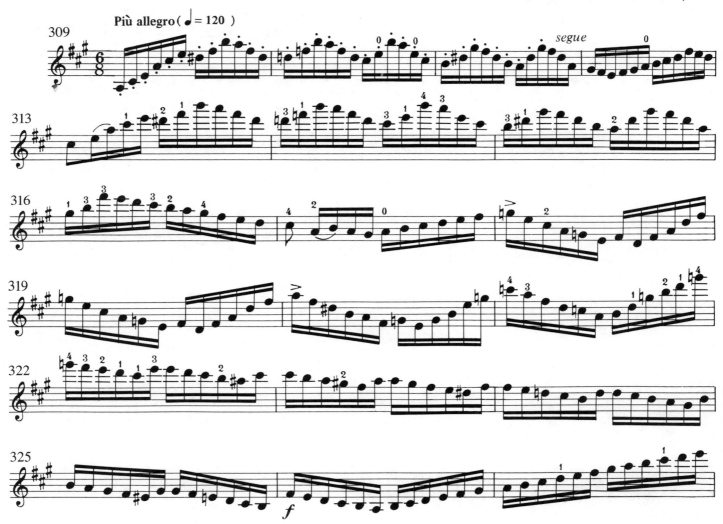

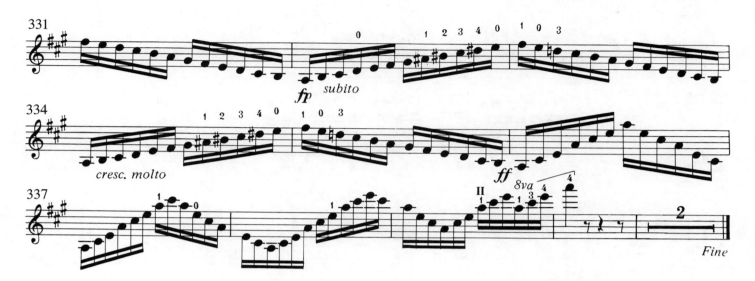

V. Pedagogical tips for **tremolo** in the <u>middle third</u> and <u>upper third</u> of the bow
  A. pronate the forearm
  B. flatten the bow hair
  C. initiate a rapid hand-shaking motion* in a direction that is diagonal to the shaft of the bow
  D. after mastering examples 7 and 8, apply these solutions to Mazas Etude No. 67 and the final measures of the Violin Concerto in E Minor, Op. 64 by Felix Mendelssohn

EXAMPLE 7

Tremolo — middle third and upper third of bow
Jacques Fereol Mazas, No. 67
open string practice
meas. 1–16

*a motion similar to enthusiastically waving goodbye to a friend

Note: In <u>slow measured tremolos</u> use less hand motion and more forearm and upper arm motion. In <u>fast measured</u> and <u>unmeasured tremolos</u> use more hand motion and less forearm and upper arm motion.

ETUDE

Jacques Fereol Mazas, No. 67

EXAMPLE 8

Tremolo — middle third of bow
Felix Mendelssohn
Violin Concerto in E Minor, Op. 64 (3rd Movement)
meas. 198–204

VIOLIN CONCERTO IN E MINOR
3rd Movement — last portion

Felix Mendelssohn,
Op. 64

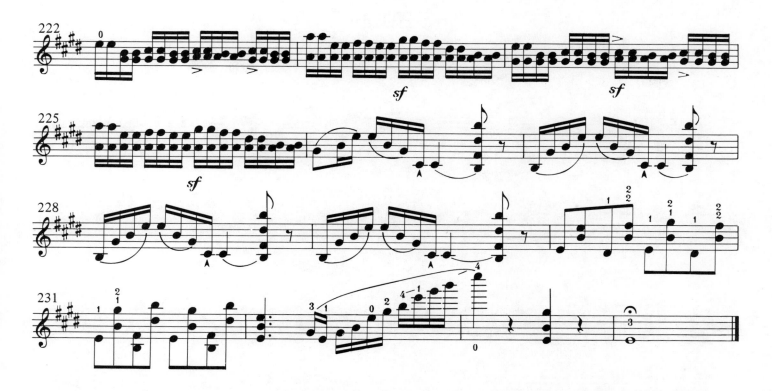

VI. Pedagogical tips for ricochet in the middle third and upper third of the bow 傾斜的

A. pronate the forearm for thrown strokes in the upper third of the bow, and supinate the forearm for thrown strokes in the middle third of the bow

B. flatten the bow hair

C. lift the first finger off the bow

D. from a height of about 2 inches, allow the bow to fall freely on the string, letting it bounce vertically on its own merit

E. add a lateral motion to the bounce and passively replace the first finger to the bow hold 被動的

側面的
橫向的

F. select the number of bounces needed

G. after mastering examples 9 and 10, apply these solutions to Mazas Etude No. 51 and Rondo Des Lutins, Op. 25 by Antonio Bazzini

EXAMPLE 9

Ricochet — middle third and upper third of bow
Jacques Fereol Mazas, No. 51
open string practice
meas. 1–8

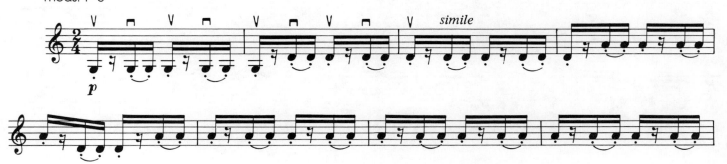

ETUDE

Jacques Fereol Mazas, No. 51

EXAMPLE 10

Ricochet — middle third and upper third of bow
Antonio Bazzini
Le Rondo Des Lutins
open string practice
meas. 5–14

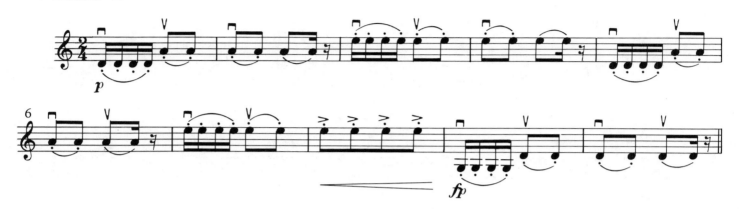

LE RONDO DES LUTINS
Opening Excerpt

Antonio Bazzini, Op. 25

a tempo

VII. Pedagogical tips for **arpeggiando saltando** in the <u>middle third</u> of the bow

    A. supinate the forearm

    B. flatten the bow hair

    C. initiate a <u>silent</u> string crossing motion from open G to open E and back again moving the entire arm as one unit from the shoulder*

    D. add just enough <u>lateral</u> motion to the bowing stroke to evenly articulate all open string sounds

    E. increase the bow speed from slow to fast until the bow begins to bounce

    F. after mastering examples 11 and 12, apply solutions to Dont Etude Op. 35, No. 19 and the excerpt from the Scene De Ballet, Op. 100 by Charles de Beriot

EXAMPLE 11

Arpeggiando Saltando — middle third of bow
Jakob Dont, Op. 35, No. 19
open string practice
meas. 1–6

*Lift the 1st (index) finger off the bow in pedagogical tips C, D and E until the desired bounce is achieved. Then passively add the 1st finger to the bow hold.

ETUDE

Jakob Dont, Op. 35, No. 19

EXAMPLE 12

Arpeggiando Saltando — middle third of bow
Charles de Beriot
Scene de Ballet, Op. 100 (Temp di Bolero)
open string practice
meas. 94–96

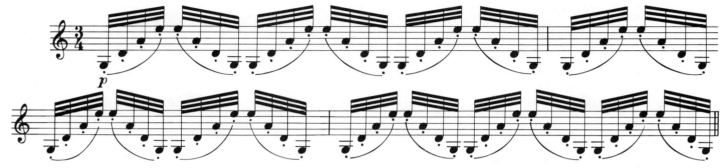

SCENE DE BALLET
Excerpt

Tempo di Bolero

Charles de Beriot, Op. 100

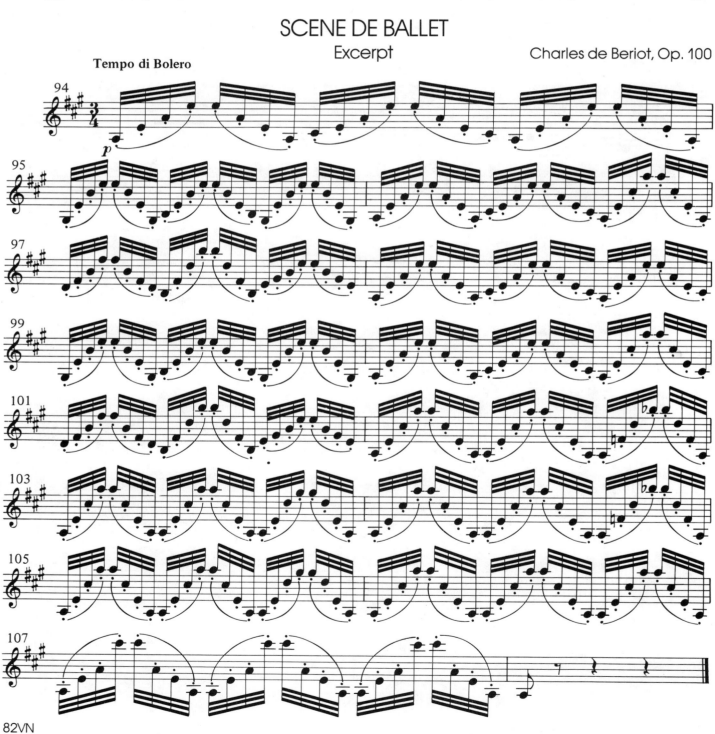

VIII. Pedagogical tips for **up bow flying spiccato** and **jeté** in the <u>middle third</u> of the bow

    A. supinate the forearm

    B. flatten the bow hair

    C. use silent vertical bowing motions on all indicated pitches, with a relaxed posture in the upper arm, forearm and hand

    D. when the rhythms and string levels are mastered, initiate a clockwise bowing motion with the right hand, keeping the wrist flexible, and <u>glancing the bow off the string from an elevation of about one inch.</u>

    E. after mastering examples 13 and 14, apply solutions to Kreutzer Etude No. 20 and Caprice, Op. 1, No. 19 by Niccolo Paganini

EXAMPLE 13

Up bow flying spiccato and Jeté — middle third of bow
Rodolphe Kreutzer, No. 20
open string practice
meas. 1–5

*The bow may either be returned to the point of origin (Jeté) or moved slightly toward the frog after each stroke (up bow flying spiccato).

ETUDE

Rodolphe Kreutzer, No. 20

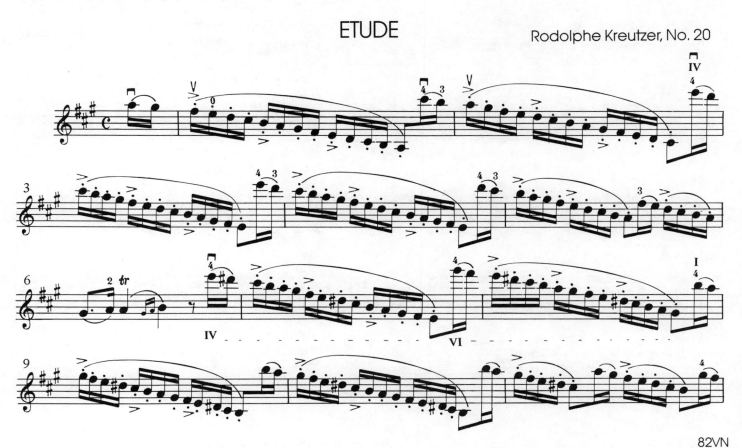

EXAMPLE 14

Up bow flying spiccato and Jeté — middle third of bow
Niccolo Paganini
Caprice, Op. 1, No. 19
open string practice
meas. 5—10

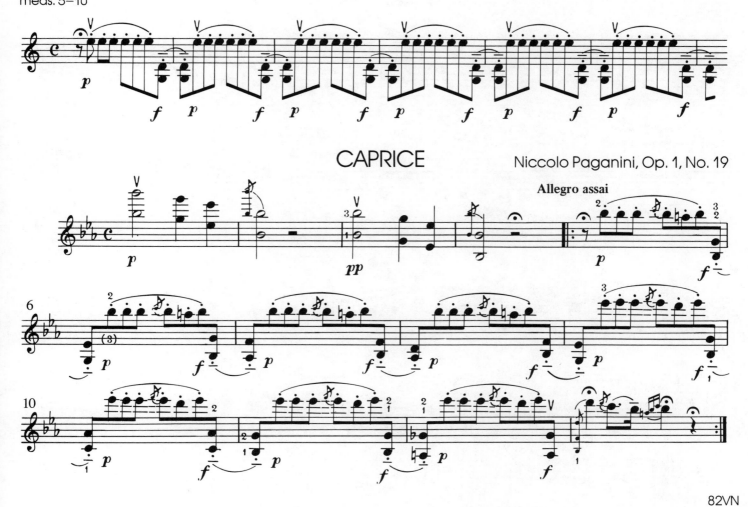

CAPRICE

Niccolo Paganini, Op. 1, No. 19

Allegro assai

UNIT THREE
Extended Hand Position

I. Description
  A. larger spaces between the first and second fingers and between the third and fourth fingers
  B. the second and third fingers are placed slightly deeper
  C. contact point with the bow is closer to the 1st crease of the index finger

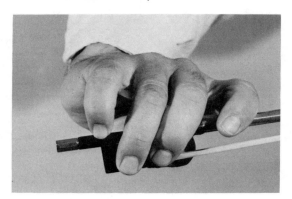 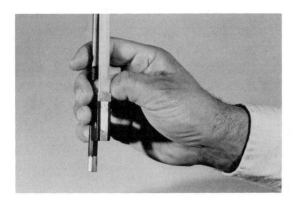

II. Ideal bowings
  A. collé in the lower third and upper two-thirds of the bow
  B. ruvido (rough) détaché in the lower third of the bow
  C. chordal playing in the lower third of the bow
  D. portato (louré) in the upper two-thirds and the lower third of the bow
III. Pedagogical tips for **collé** in the <u>lower third</u> and the <u>upper two-thirds</u> of the bow
  A. supinate the forearm in the lower third and pronate the forearm in the upper two-thirds of the bow
  B. tilt the bow shaft toward the fingerboard in the lower third of the bow and flatten the bow hair in the upper two-thirds of the bow
  C. place the bow on the string and silently 'rock' the string from right to left using the natural weight of the arm
  D. initiate down and up bow motions by releasing each placed stroke with great speed using the fingers, hand and forearm, but with most of the activity occurring in the fingers
  E. at each release, the string will be 'pinched' and the bow will reset for the next 'pinch'
  F. release each stroke in an arched direction similar to that of the bow shaft
  G. after mastering examples 15 and 16, apply solutions to Dont Etude Op. 35, No. 16 and excerpts from the fourth movement of Sonata in C Minor, Op. 30. No. 2 by Ludwig van Beethoven

Collé — lower third of bow
Jakob Dont, Op. 35, No. 16
open string practice
meas. 1–6

EXAMPLE 15

ETUDE

Jakob Dont, Op. 35, No. 16

40

82VN

EXAMPLE 16

Collé — lower third of bow
Ludwig van Beethoven
Sonata in C Minor, Op. 30, No. 2 (4th mvt.)
meas. 40–53

SONATA IN C MINOR
Excerpt

Ludwig van Beethoven,
Op. 30, No. 2

IV. Pedgagical tips for ruvido (rough) détaché in the <u>lower third</u> of the bow

    A. supinate the forearm

    B. tilt the bow shaft slightly toward the fingerboard

    C. lean into the string with the natural weight of the arm

    D. initiate fast down and up bow motions

        1. with a relaxed posture of the right arm

        2. with flexibility in the thumb, fingers, hand and wrist

    E. after mastering examples 17 and 18, apply solutions to Fiorillo Etude No. 21 and excerpts from Zigeunerweisen, Op. 20 by Sarasate, Tarantelle, Op. 6 by Wieniawski and Concertstücke, Op. 20 by Saint-Saëns

EXAMPLE 17

Ruvido (rough) détaché — lower third of bow
Federigo Fiorillo, No. 21
open string practice
meas. 1–6

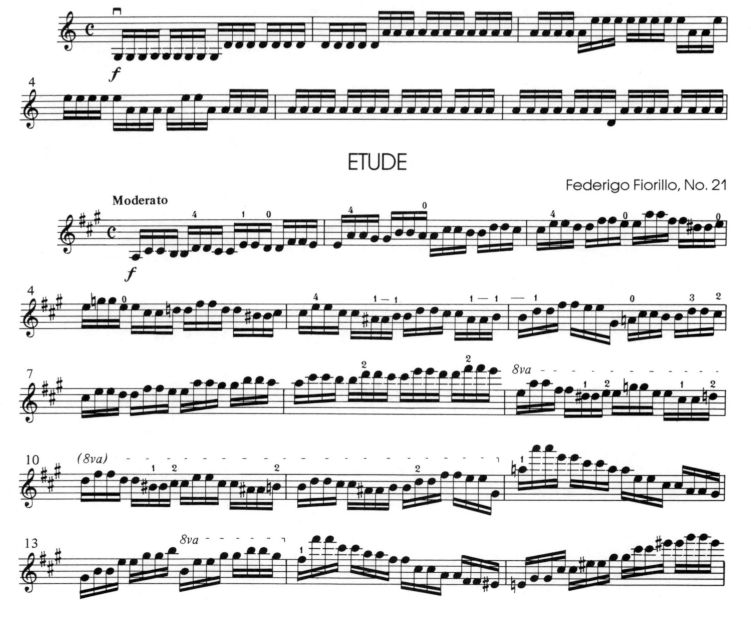

ETUDE

Federigo Fiorillo, No. 21

EXAMPLE 18

Ruvido détaché — lower third of bow
Pablo de Sarasate
Zigeunerweisen, Op. 20
open string practice
meas. 138-145

ZIGEUNERWEISEN
Excerpt
Pablo de Sarasate, Op. 20

Allegro molto vivace

44

SCHERZO TARANTELLE
Excerpts

Henri Wieniawski, Op. 6

CONCERTSTÜCKE
Excerpt

Camille Saint-Saëns, Op. 20

V. Pedagogical tips for **chordal playing** in the <u>lower third</u> of the bow
  A. pronate the forearm
  B. flatten the bow hair
  C. place the bow on the string closer to the fingerboard than to the bridge
  D. add enough arm weight until the hair of the bow is in contact with the notes of each string
  E. maintain a firm grip on the bow by pressing the thumb up against the bow shaft
  F. release consecutive down bows with quick circular counter-clockwise motions, 'kicking' the right elbow upward with each stroke
  G. after mastering examples 19 and 20, apply solutions to Dont Etude Op. 35, No. 1 and the Fugue from the Unaccompanied Sonata in A Minor by Johann Sebastian Bach

EXAMPLE 19

Chordal playing—lower third of bow
Jakob Dont, Op. 35, No. 1
open string practice
meas. 1–14

ETUDE

Jakob Dont, Op. 35, No. 1

EXAMPLE 20

Chordal playing — lower third of bow
Johann Sebastian Bach
Sonata in A Minor for Solo Violin (Fuga)
open string practice
meas. 7–13

SONATA IN A MINOR FOR SOLO VIOLIN
Fuga — Excerpts

Johann Sebastian Bach

VI. Pedagogical tips for **portato** (louré) in the <u>upper two-thirds</u> and the <u>lower third</u> of the bow
   A. pronate the forearm in the upper two-thirds of the bow and supinate the forearm in the lower third of the bow
   B. flatten the bow hair in the upper two-thirds of the bow and tilt the bow shaft slightly toward the fingerboard in the lower third of the bow
   C. using the natural weight and leverage of the right arm, silently dip the shaft of the bow into the hair
   D. draw a whole bow dipping slightly on the accented notes of examples 21 and 22 until smoothly pulsating articulations are achieved
   E. add intensity to the sound by pulsating the right thumb up against the bow shaft with each dip
   F. after mastering examples 21 and 22, apply solutions to Rode Etude No. 18 and the second movement of the Concerto for Two Violins in D Minor by Johann Sebastian Bach

EXAMPLE 21

Portato (Louré) — upper two-thirds and lower third of bow
Pierre Rode, No. 18
open string practice
meas. 1–11

ETUDE

Pierre Rode, No. 18

EXAMPLE 22

Portato (Louré) — upper two-thirds and lower third of bow
Johann Sebastian Bach
Concerto in D Minor to Two Violins (2nd Mvt.)
open string practice
meas. 1–7

CONCERTO IN D MINOR FOR TWO VIOLINS
2nd Movement
Johann Sebastian Bach

UNIT FOUR
Extended Hand Position

I. Description

    A. larger spaces between the first and second fingers and between the third and fourth fingers

    B. the second and third fingers are placed slightly deeper

    C. contact point with the bow is closer to the second crease of the index finger

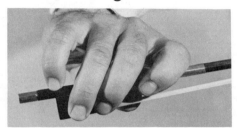 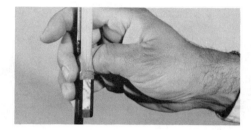

II. Ideal bowings

    A. martelé in the upper two-thirds and lower third of the bow

    B. fast up bow staccato in the upper two-thirds and lower third of the bow

    C. slow staccato in the upper two-thirds and lower third of the bow

    D. smooth détaché in the upper two-thirds and lower third of the bow

    E. accented détaché (Serré) in the lower third, middle third and upper third of the bow

    F. expressive détaché (détaché chanté or détaché porté) in the lower third, middle third and upper third of the bow

    G. fouetté détaché (whipped détaché) in the middle third of the bow

    H. lance détaché (speared détaché) — short, quick thrusts on the string in the upper third of the bow

    I. sustained whole bow stroke (son filé)

    J. legato string crossings

    K. détaché string crossings in the middle third of the bow

III. Pedagogical tips for **martelé** in the <u>upper two-thirds</u> and lower third of the bow

    A. <u>pronate</u> the forearm in the upper two-thirds of the bow and <u>supinate</u> the forearm in the lower third of the bow

    B. flatten the bow hair in the upper two-thirds of the bow and tilt the bow shaft slightly toward the fingerboard in the lower third of the bow

    C. lift the second and third fingers off the bow and <u>press the thumb upward against the bow shaft</u>

    D. silently rock the string from right to left using the natural weight of the arm

    E. <u>release each stroke quickly</u> in a slightly <u>arched</u> direction similar to that of the shaft of the bow*

    F. when the rhythms and string levels are mastered, replace the 2nd and 3rd fingers to the bow hold and apply these solutions to Fiorillo Etude No. 15 and the excerpt from the second movement of the Sonata in D Major by George Frederic Handel

EXAMPLE 23

Martelé—upper two-thirds of bow
Federigo Fiorillo, No. 15
open string practice
meas. 1–8

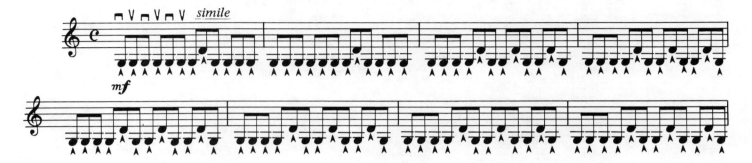

*Although the Martelé may be executed at any point of the bow, it will sound best where the bow is
stiffest, most often in the upper and lower thirds of the bow.

ETUDE

Federigo Fiorillo, No. 15

EXAMPLE 24

Martelé — upper two-thirds of bow
George Frederic Handel
Sonata in D Major (2nd Mvt.)
open string practice
meas. 1–5, 17–20

SONATA IN D MAJOR
2nd Movement

George Frederic Handel

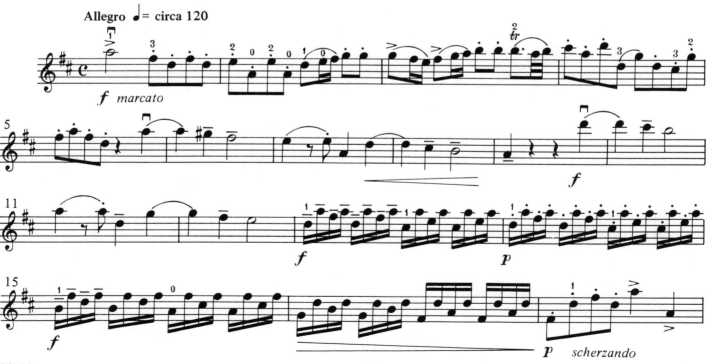

IV. Pedagogical tips for **fast up bow staccato** in the <u>upper two-thirds</u> and the <u>lower third</u> of the bow

    A. pronate the forearm in the upper two thirds of the bow and supinate the forearm in the lower third of the bow

    B. flatten the bow hair in the upper two-thirds of the bow and tilt the bow shaft toward the fingerboard in the lower third of the bow

    C. pull the third finger in toward the palm of the hand and press the thumb upward against the bow shaft

    D. keeping the hand flexible, initiate a quivering, tremolo motion propelled by the elbow moving the bow from the tip to the lower third

    E. adjust the speed of the bow as it moves from the tip to the frog until the down bow articulations of the tremolo are eliminated*

    F. after mastering examples 25 and 26, apply solutions to Kreutzer Etude No. 4 and Caprice in G Minor, Op. 1, No. 10 by Niccolo Paganini

EXAMPLE 25

Fast Up Bow Staccato — upper two-thirds and lower third of bow
Rodolphe Kreutzer, No. 4
open string practice
meas. 1–10

*Move the bow diagonally across the strings with the tip aimed toward the fingerboard.

ETUDE

Rodolphe Kreutzer, No. 4

EXAMPLE 26

Fast Up Bow Staccato — upper two-thirds and lower third of bow
Niccolo Paganini
Caprice in G Minor, Op. 1, No. 10
open string practice
meas. 1–6

CAPRICE

Niccolo Paganini, Op. 1, No. 10

V. Pedagogical tips for **slow staccato** in the <u>upper two-thirds</u> and <u>lower third</u> of the bow

   A. pronate the forearm in the upper two-thirds of the bow and supinate the forearm in the lower third of the bow

   B. flatten the bow hair in the upper two-thirds of the bow and tilt the bow shaft slightly toward the fingerboard in the lower third of the bow

   C. pull the third finger in toward the palm of the hand and press the thumb gently up against the bow shaft

   D. keeping the hand flexible, <u>initiate a series of</u> martelé-type strokes by first using consecutive down and up bow motions and then incorporating these same articulations within extended slurs

   E. use the spaces between notes to prepare succeeding articulations and to place the fingers of the left hand

   F. after mastering examples 27 and 28, apply these solutions to Mazas Etude No. 29 and the second violin part of the Andante Espressivo movement from the String Quartet in D Major, Op. 44, No. 1 by Felix Mendelssohn

EXAMPLE 27

Slow Staccato — upper two-thirds and lower third of bow
Jacques Fereol Mazas, No. 29
open string practice
meas. 1–8

ETUDE

Jacques Fereol Mazas, No. 29

EXAMPLE 28

Slow Staccato — upper two-thirds and lower third of bow
Felix Mendelssohn
String Quartet in D Major, Op. 44, No. 1 (2nd Mvt., 2nd Violin part)
meas. 1–10

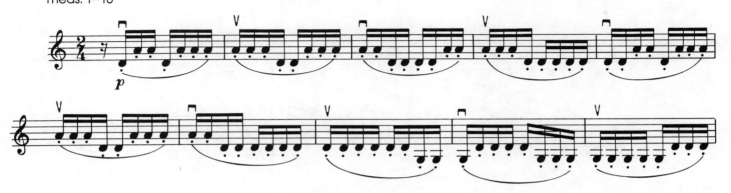

STRING QUARTET IN D MAJOR
2nd Movement — 2nd Violin part

Felix Mendelssohn,
Op. 44, No. 1

62

82VN

VI. Pedagogical tips for **smooth détaché** in the <u>upper two-thirds</u> and <u>lower third</u> of the bow
   A. pronate the forearm in the upper two-thirds of the bow and supinate the forearm in the lower third of the bow
   B. flatten the bow hair in the upper two-thirds of the bow and tilt the bow shaft toward the fingerboard in the lower third of the bow
   C. maintain a relaxed passive posture in the fingers
   D. initiate the stroke with the forearm and upper arm
     1. keep a steady amount of weight in contact with the string
     2. execute the changes of bow direction without increasing the bow speed
   E. follow the arch of the shaft of the bow in both up and down bow motions
   F. after mastering examples 29 and 30, apply solutions to Fiorillo Etude No. 11 and the Double from the Partita in B Minor for Solo Violin by Johann Sebastian Bach

EXAMPLE 29

Smooth Détaché — upper two-thirds and lower third of bow
Federigo Fiorillo, No. 11
open string practice
meas. 1–6

*In slower speeds, the smooth détaché uses more upper arm and forearm motion and less hand motion.
In faster speeds, the smooth détaché uses more hand motion and less upper arm and forearm motion.

ETUDE

Federigo Fiorillo, No. 11

EXAMPLE 30

Smooth Détaché — upper two-thirds and lower third of bow
Johann Sebastian Bach
Double from Partita No. 2 in D Minor
open string practice
meas. 1–8

PARTITA NO. 2 IN D MINOR FOR SOLO VIOLIN
Double

Johann Sebastian Bach

VII. Pedagogical tips for **accented détaché** (serré) in the <u>lower third</u>, the <u>middle third</u>, and <u>upper third</u> of the bow
  A. supinate the forearm in the lower third of the bow and pronate the forearm in the middle third and upper third of the bow
  B. tilt the bow shaft slightly toward the fingerboard in the lower third and flatten the bow hair in the upper two-thirds of the bow
  C. keep a relaxed passive posture in the fingers of the right hand
  D. initiate the bow stroke with the upper arm and forearm
  E. directly at the point of change from down bow to up bow, flip the fingers into an extended position and directly at the point of change from up to down bow, flip the fingers into a closed position
  F. after mastering examples 31 and 32, apply solutions to Rode Etude No. 8 and the excerpt from the Concerto for Two Violins in D Minor by Antonio Vivaldi

EXAMPLE 31

Accented Détaché (Serré) — lower third, middle third and upper third of bow
Pierre Rode, No. 8
open string practice
meas. 1–4

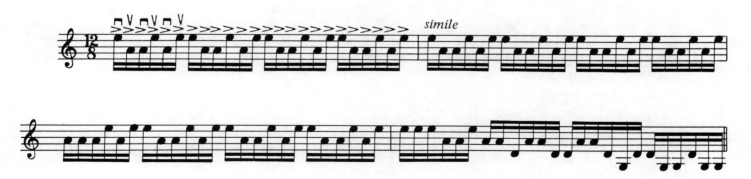

*When the Accented Détaché is executed with the whole bow it is called "Le Grand Détaché."

ETUDE

Pierre Rode, No. 8

EXAMPLE 32

Accented Détaché (Serré) — middle of bow
Antonio Vivaldi
Concerto in D Minor for Two Violins, Op. 3,
No. 11 (3rd Mvt., 1st Violin part)
open string practice
meas. 1-7, 14-16

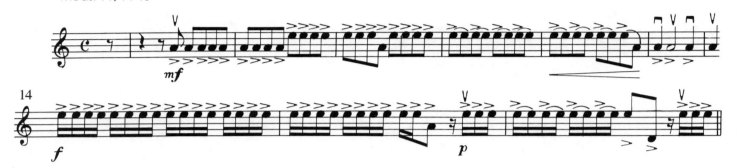

CONCERTO IN D MINOR FOR TWO VIOLINS
3rd Movement — 1st Violin part

Antonio Vivaldi,
Op. 3, No. 11

VIII. Pedagogical tips for **expressive détaché** (détaché chanté or
    détaché porté) in the <u>lower third</u>, <u>middle third</u> and <u>upper third</u> of
    the bow
  A. supinate the forearm in the lower third of the bow and pronate
    the forearm in the middle third and upper third of the bow
  B. tilt the bow shaft slightly toward the fingerboard in the lower third
    and flatten the bow hair in the upper two-thirds of the bow
  C. execute slow, smooth, unaccented détaché strokes in various
    parts of the bow aiming for an even bow speed
  D. at the point of each bow change, add a slight increase of speed
    and weight by dipping the bow shaft into the bow hair producing
    an expressive, cushiony accent
  E. after mastering examples 33 and 34, apply solutions to Mazas
    Etude No. 5 and the third movement of the Sonata for Violin and
    Piano, Op. 5, No. 4 by Arcangelo Corelli

EXAMPLE 33

Expressive Détaché (Détache Chanté or Détaché Porté) — lower third, middle third
and upper third of bow
Jacques Fereol Mazas, No. 5
open string practice
meas. 1–4

ETUDE

Jacques Fereol Mazas, No. 5

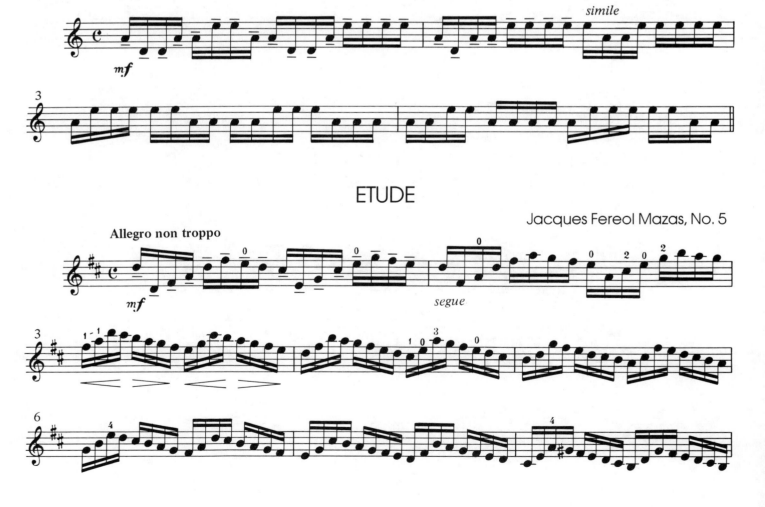

EXAMPLE 34

Expressive Détaché (Détaché Chanté or Détaché Porté) — lower third, middle third
and upper third of bow
Arcangelo Corelli
Sonata for Violin and Piano, Op. 5, No. 4
(3rd Mvt.)
meas. 1–8

SONATA FOR VIOLIN AND PIANO
3rd Movement

Arcangelo Corelli,
Op. 5, No. 4

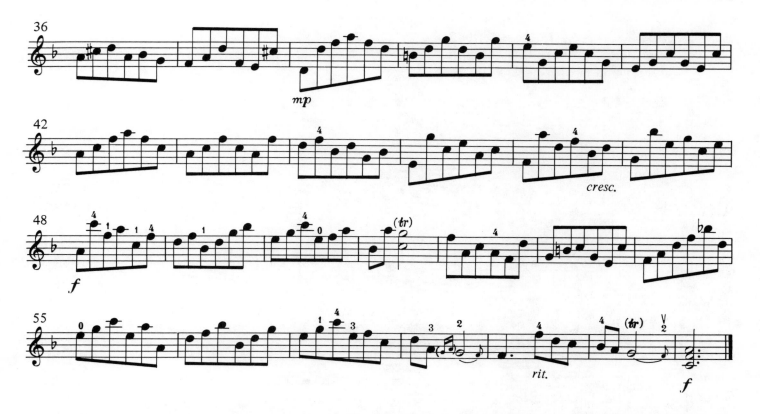

IX. Pedagogical tips for **fouetté détaché** (whipped détaché) in the
<u>middle third</u> of the bow
   A. pronate the forearm
   B. flatten the bow hair
   C. maintain a firm grip with all fingers of the right hand
   D. using the natural weight and leverage of the whole arm, initiate a
      silent 'whipping' motion of the bow shaft into the bow hair
   E. draw short fast down and up bows, keeping the bow from jumping
      too far off the string
   F. after mastering examples 35 and 36, apply solutions to Kreutzer
      Etude No. 2 and the Fugue from the Sonata in C Minor for
      Unaccompanied Violin by Johann Sebastian Bach

EXAMPLE 35

Fouetté Détaché (Whipped Détaché) — middle third of bow
Rodolphe Kreutzer, No. 2
open string practice
meas. 1–4

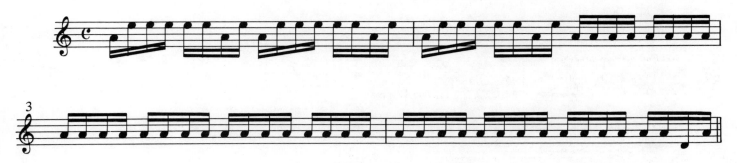

ETUDE

Rodolphe Kreutzer, No. 2

Allegro moderato

EXAMPLE 36

Fouetté Détaché (Whipped Détaché) — middle third of bow
Johann Sebastian Bach
Sonata in C Major for Unaccompanied Violin (Fugue)
open string practice
meas. 165–172

SONATA IN C MAJOR FOR SOLO VIOLIN
Fugue — Excerpts

Johann Sebastian Bach

X. Pedagogical tips for **lance détaché** (speared détaché)-short
   quick thrusts on the string in the <u>upper third</u> of the bow
   A. supinate the forearm for a soft sound, pronate slightly for a
      stronger sound
   B. flatten the bow hair
   C. lift the second and third fingers off the bow and press the thumb
      up against the bow shaft
   D. without any accents and with great speed, execute down and up
      bows using a whole arm motion
   E. draw each stroke in a slightly arched direction similar to that of the
      shaft of the bow
   F. passively replace the second and third fingers to the bow hold
   G. after mastering examples 37 and 38, apply solutions to Fiorillo
      Etude No. 34 and the second movement of the Concerto in B
      Minor, Opus 61 by Camille Saint-Saëns

EXAMPLE 37

Lance Détaché (Speared Détaché)-short, quick thrusts on
string, upper third of bow
Federigo Fiorillo, No. 34
open string practice
meas. 1-4

ETUDE

Federigo Fiorillo, No. 34

EXAMPLE 38

Lance Détaché (Speared Détaché)-short, quick thrusts on
string, upper third of bow
Camille Saint-Saëns-Concerto in B Minor, Op. 61 (2nd Mvt.)
open string practice
meas. 37-38, 140-143

CONCERTO IN B MINOR
2nd Movement

Camille Saint-Saëns, Op. 61

XI. Pedadogical tips for **sustained whole bow stroke** (son filé)
    A. supinate the forearm in the lower third of the bow and pronate
       the forearm in the upper two thirds of the bow
    B. tilt the bow shaft slightly toward the fingerboard in the lower third
       of the bow and flatten the bow hair in the upper two thirds of
       the bow
    C. using the natural weight of the right arm, draw the bow in a plane
       parallel to the bridge
    D. to develop an intense sound, pull the third finger in toward the
       palm of the hand throughout each stroke
    E. during soft sustained bow strokes the bow changes are executed with
       the fingers and during loud sustained bow strokes the bow changes are
       executed with the forearm
    F. after mastering examples 39 and 40, apply solutions to Fiorillo
       Etude No. 15 and the second movement of the Concerto in D
       Minor, Opus 22 by Henri Wieniawski

EXAMPLE 39

Sustained Whole Bow Stroke (Son Filé)
Federigo Fiorillo, No. 14
open string practice
meas. 1–8

ETUDE

Federigo Fiorillo, No. 14

EXAMPLE 40

Sustained Whole Bow Stroke (Son Filé)
Henri Wieniawski
Concerto No. 2 in D Minor, Op 22 (2nd Mvt.)
open string practice
meas. 1–8

CONCERTO NO. 2 IN D MINOR
2nd Movement

Henri Wieniawski, Op. 22

84

82VN

XII. Pedagogical tips for **legato string crossings**
   A. supinate the forearm
   B. place the bow on any open string and lift the first finger off
      the bow
   C. maintain a relaxed posture in the upper right arm
   D. initiate vertical waving motions of the right forearm while drawing
      consecutive down and up bows on one string without sounding
      any of the adjacent strings*
   E. using these same motions and with the first finger resting passively
      on the bow, add the sound of an adjacent string
   F. maintain flexibility in the right elbow to anticipate smooth string
      level changes
   G. to eliminate exaggerated motions, stay close to those strings
      being sounded
   H. after mastering examples 41 and 42, apply solutions to Rode
      Etude No. 3 and the first movement of the Sonata in D Minor, Op.
      108 by Johannes Brahms

EXAMPLE 41

Legato String Crossings
Pierre Rode, No. 3
open string practice
meas. 1–6

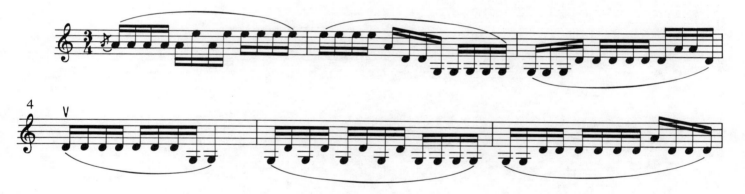

*In fast string crossings, more hand is used, in slow string crossings, more forearm is used.

ETUDE

Pierre Rode, No. 3

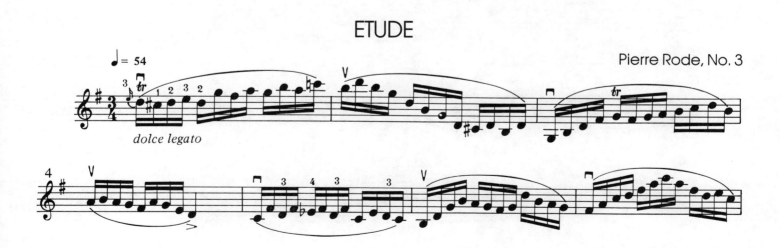

EXAMPLE 42

Legato String Crossings
Johannes Brahms
Sonata in D Minor, Op. 108 (1st Mvt.)
open string practice
meas. 84–87, 96–99

SONATA IN D MINOR
1st Movement — Excerpt
Johannes Brahms, Op. 108

molto *p* e mezza voce sempre

XIII. Pedagogical tips for **détaché string crossings** in the <u>middle third</u> of the bow
   A. supinate the forearm
   B. flatten the bow hair and place the bow on the G string
   C. maintain a relaxed posture in the upper right arm
   D. initiate circular clockwise motions of the right forearm, drawing consecutive down and up bows on the G string only
   E. expand these circular clockwise motions to include the D string on the up bows
   F. to eliminate exaggerated motions, stay close to both sounding strings
   G. after mastering examples 43 and 44, apply solutions to Dont Etude No. 5 and the fourth movement of Sonata in G Minor for Solo Violin by Johann Sebastian Bach

EXAMPLE 43

Détaché String Crossings
Jakob Dont Op. 35, No. 5
open string practice
meas. 1 and 5

ETUDE

Jakob Dont Op. 35, No. 5

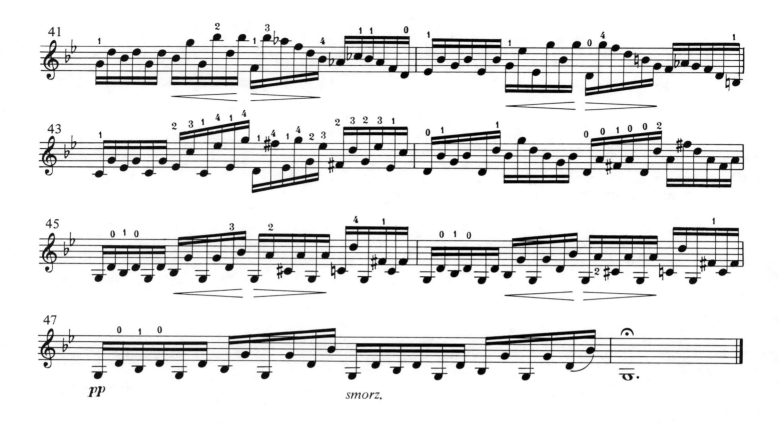

EXAMPLE 44

Détaché String Crossings*
Johann Sebastian Bach
Sonata in G Minor for Solo Violin (4th Mvt.)
open string practice
meas. 1–4, 17–20

*In example 44 use a counterclockwise circular forearm motion.

SONATA IN G MINOR FOR SOLO VIOLIN
4th Movement — Excerpt

Johann Sebastian Bach

82VN

UNIT 5
Additional Bowing Articulations

I. Bariolage
   A. Description
      1. French-meaning "medley of colors"
      2. stopped notes and open string notes consecutively interchanged within a recurring bowing pattern
      3. utilizes natural hand position described in Unit Two
   B. Pedagogical tips for **bariolage**
      1. supinate the forearm
      2. flatten the bow hair and place bow at the mid-point
      3. using the whole arm, silently rock the bow from the double stop A and E string level to the double stop D and A string level
      4. maintaining the same whole arm motion, sound the notes of example 45 by adding a flexible, lateral forearm détaché
      5. incorporate same movements in example 46
      6. when properly executed, this stroke will utilize a vertical motion in the upper arm and a lateral motion in the forearm
      7. after mastering examples 45 and 46, apply solutions to the Preludio from the Partita in E Major for Unaccompanied Violin by Johann Sebastian Bach

EXAMPLE 45

Bariolage
Johann Sebastian Bach
Partita in E Major for Solo Violin (Preludio)
open string practice
meas. 17–20

EXAMPLE 46

PARTITA IN E MAJOR FOR SOLO VIOLIN
Preludio-Excerpt

Johann Sebastian Bach

To facilitate page turns a blank page has been added.

82VN

II. Mixed Bowings — Recovery-type bowing patterns
  A. Description
    1. rhythmic patterns in which slurred groupings are always in the same bowing direction
    2. utilizes natural hand position described in Unit Four
  B. Pedagogical tips for **recovery-type bowing** patterns
    1. pronate the forearm
    2. flatten the bow hair and place the bow in the middle third
    3. use exactly the same amount of bow for the slurred groupings as for the separate notes
    4. to achieve this, the bow speed must be three times as slow on the slurred groupings as for the separate notes in examples 47–49
    5. in example 50, the bow speed must be twice as slow on slurred groupings as for the separate notes
    6. after mastering examples 47–50, apply solutions to the musical fragments from the Concerto in A Minor by Johann Sebastian Bach, the Caprice, Op. 1, No. 15 by Niccolo Paganini and the Violin Concerto in D Major, Op. 61 by Ludwig van Beethoven

EXAMPLE 47

Mixed Bowings — recovery-type bowing patterns
Johann Sebastian Bach
Concerto in A Minor (1st Mvt.)
open string practice
meas. 29–32

EXAMPLE 48

meas. 88-91

CONCERTO IN A MINOR
1st Movement — Excerpt

Johann Sebastian Bach

EXAMPLE 49

Mixed Bowings-Recovery-Type Bowing Patterns
Niccolo Paganini
Caprice, Op. 1, No. 15
open string practice
meas. 8–11

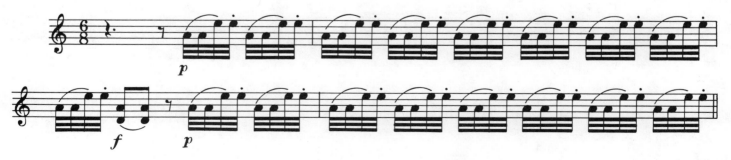

CAPRICE
Excerpt

Niccolo Paganini, Op. 1, No. 15

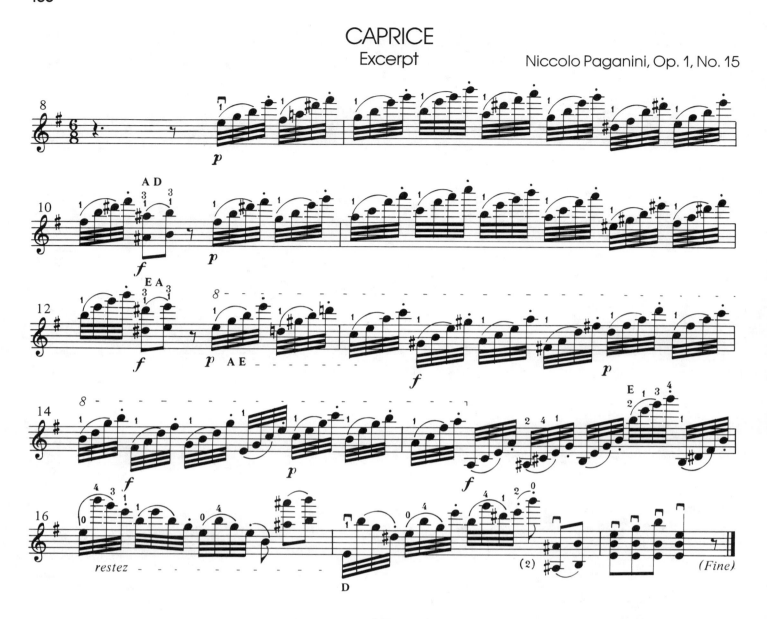

EXAMPLE 50

Mixed Bowings-Recovery-Type Bowing Patterns
Ludwig van Beethoven
Concerto in D Major, Opus 61 (1st Mvt.)
open string practice
meas. 134–137

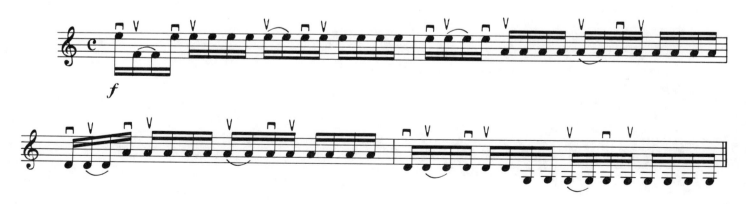

CONCERTO IN D MAJOR

1st Movement — Excerpt

Ludwig van Beethoven, Op. 61

III. Mixed Bowings—Alternation-type bowing patterns
  A. Description
    1. rhythmic patterns in which slurred groupings are alternately in a down and up bow direction
    2. utilize Natural Hand Position described in Unit Two
  B. Pedagogical tips for **alternation-type bowing** patterns
    1. pronate the forearm
    2. flatten bow hair and place bow in the middle third
    3. use more bow on slurred groupings than for the separate notes
    4. to achieve this, maintain the same bow speed for the slurred groupings as for the separate notes. This will insure remaining in the same bow area for the entire passage
    5. after mastering examples 51 and 52, apply solutions to the musical fragments from the Sonata in A Major ("Kreutzer"), Op. 47 by Ludwig van Beethoven and the Sonata in G Major, Op. 30 also by Beethoven

EXAMPLE 51

Mixed Bowings-Alternation-Type Bowing Patterns
Ludwig van Beethoven
Sonata in A Major ("Kreutzer"), Op. 47 (2nd Mvt.)
open string practice
meas. 1–4

EXAMPLE 52

Mixed Bowings-Alternation-Type Bowing Patterns
Ludwig van Beethoven
Sonata in G Major, Op. 30, no. 3 (3rd Mvt.)
open string practice
meas. 12–15

SONATA IN A MAJOR ("Kreutzer")
2nd Movement — Variation II

Ludwig van Beethoven, Op. 47

SONATA IN G MAJOR
3rd Movement — Excerpt

Ludwig van Beethoven, Op. 30, No. 3

UNIT SIX
General Pedagogical Considerations

The step-by-step rules provided on the previous pages for the vast styles of bowing articulations must also be accompanied by the following general considerations in order to produce the best tonal results.

I. Bow-String Contact point
    A. further from the bridge on the lower open strings
    B. closer to the bridge on the higher open strings
    C. further from the bridge on longer string lengths
    D. closer to the bridge on shorter string lengths

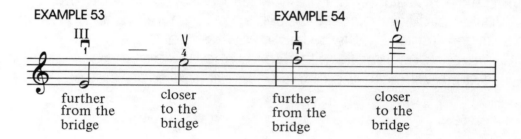

II. Bow Pressure
    A. lighter when playing near the fingerboard
    B. weightier when playing near the bridge
III. Bow Pressure for specific instances
    A. weightier on longer string lengths in solid double stop combinations; viz., 3rds, 6ths, 8ths and 10ths. (see examples 55–58)

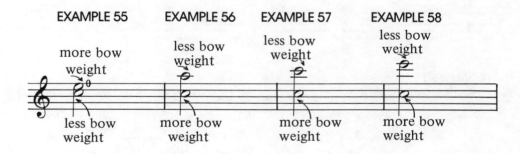

    B. weightier on the longer string lengths in double stop combinations involving trills (see examples 59–62)

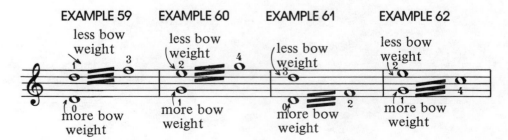

C. lighter and closer to the bridge for executing single natural or artificial harmonics (tilted bow hair is desirable for single and double harmonics)

D. lighter for artificial harmonics when they are used in double stop combinations with natural harmonics (see examples 63 and 64)

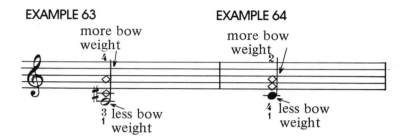

IV. Practice Procedure for Lateral Bowing Strokes on repeated notes

A. utilize circular counterclockwise motions when starting down bow

B. utilize circular clockwise motions when starting down bow

C. utilize arched motions that follow the curve of the bow shaft rather than the straight line of the bow hair (see examples 65-68)

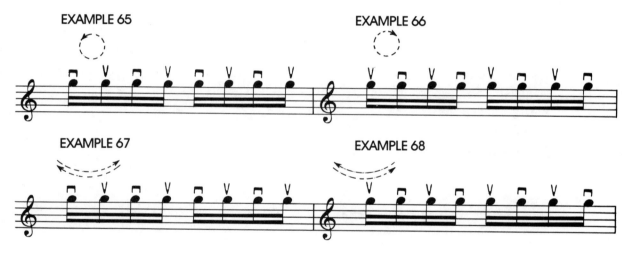

V. Bow Speed

Special Note: Altering the speed of bowing strokes is essential for clearer articulations of specific rhythmic patterns and for adding life and vitality to musical expression.

A. for melodic phrases of unequal note values, the expression of which involves the use of whole bows, the bow speed of the shorter note values must be faster and lighter than that of the longer note values (see examples 69 and 70)

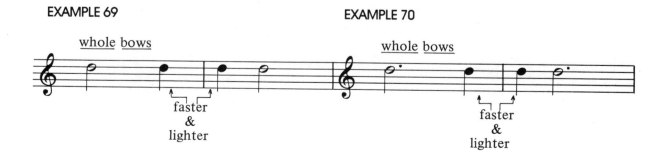

B. for melodic phrases in which inflectional swelling and subsiding is desired, increase and decrease the bow speed (see examples 71 and 72)

C. for melodic phrases where emphasis is needed to point out an important note, increase the bow speed prior to reaching that note (see example 73)

D. for melodic phrases where specific accents are needed for trills, accented grace notes, and schleifers (2 or more consecutive grace notes), increase the bow speed (see examples 74-76)

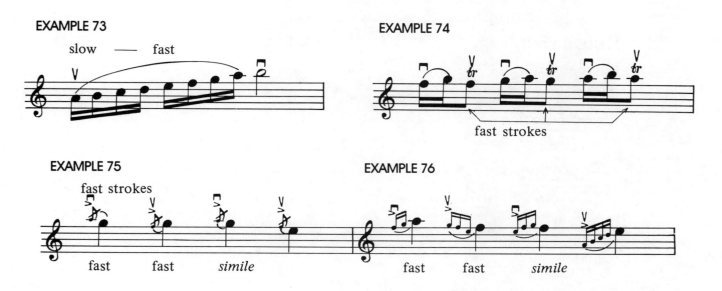

E. for melodic phrases in which slurred notes are followed by separate dotted notes, a fast thrown bow on both the slurred and separate groups insures the clear articulation of each (see examples 77–78)

F. for melodic phrases on thicker strings (G and D), the bow speed is slower and the bow pressure is weightier

G. for melodic phrases on the thinner strings (A and E), the bow speed is faster and the bow pressure is lighter

INDEX OF BOWINGS

	Page
Arpeggiando Saltando	29
Bariolage	94
Chordal Playing	45
Collé	38
Détaché	
Accented (Sérré)	67
Expressive (Chanté, Porté)	72
Fouetté (Whipped)	75
Lancé (Speared)	78
Smooth (Unaccented)	63
Ruvido (Rough)	42
Détaché String Crossings	89
General Pedagogical Considerations	105
Legato String Crossings	85
Martelé	52
Mixed Bowings	
Alternation-Type Patterns	102
Recovery-Type Patterns	97
Portato (Louré)	47
Ricochet	25
Sautillé	17
Spiccato	
Controlled (Lower third of the bow)	8
Controlled (Middle third of the bow)	12
Up Bow Flying Spiccato and the Jeté	33
Staccato	
Fast Up Bow	55
Slow	59
Sustained Whole Bow Stroke (Son Filé)	82
Tremolo	21

INDEX OF COMPOSERS AND COMPOSITIONS

Page

Bach, Johann Sebastian (1685–1750)
Concerto in A Minor (1st Movement) 98
Concerto in D Minor for Two Violins (2nd Movement) 50
Partita in D Minor for Solo Violin (Double) 66
Partita in E Major for Solo Violin (Preludio) 95
Sonata in A Minor for Solo Violin (Fuga) 46
Sonata in C Major for Solo Violin (Fugue) 77
Sonata in G Minor for Solo Violin (4th Movement) 93

Bazzini, Antonio (1818–1897)
Le Rondo Des Lutins 28

Beethoven, Ludwig van (1770–1827)
Concerto in D Major, Op. 61 (1st Movement) 101
Sonata in A Major, Op. 47 (2nd Movement) 103
Sonata in C Minor, Op. 30, No. 2 (4th Movement) 41
Sonata in G Major, Op. 30, No. 3 (3rd Movement) 104
String Quartet in C Minor, Op. 18, No. 4 (2nd Movement) 15

Beriot, Charles de (1883–1914)
Scene de Ballet, Op. 100 32

Brahms, Johannes (1833–1897)
Sonata in D Minor, Op. 108 (1st Movement) 88

Corelli, Arcangelo (1653–1713)
Sonata in F Major, Op. 5, No. 4 (3rd Movement) 74

Dont, Jakob (1815–1888)
Etude, Op. 35, No. 1 45
Etude, Op. 35, No. 5 90
Etude, Op. 35, No. 16 39
Etude, Op. 35, No. 19 30

Fiorillo, Federigo (1755–?)
Etude, No. 11 64
Etude, No. 14 82
Etude, No. 15 53
Etude, No. 21 42
Etude, No. 34 78

Handel, George Frederic (1685–1759)
Sonata in D Major (2nd Movement) 54

Kreutzer, Rodolphe (1766–1831)
Etude, No. 2 76
Etude, No. 4 56
Etude, No. 9 18
Etude, No. 20 33

Mazas, Jacques Fereol (1782–1849)
Etude, No. 5 72
Etude, No. 25 9
Etude, No. 29 60
Etude, No. 51 26
Etude, No. 67 22

Mendelssohn, Felix (1809–1847)
String Quartet in D Major, Op. 44, No. 1 (2nd Movement) 61
Violin Concerto in E Minor, Op. 64 (3rd Movement) 24

Paganini, Niccolo (1782–1840)
Caprice in E Minor, Op. 1, No. 15 100
Caprice in Eb Major, Op. 1, No. 19 35
Caprice in G Minor, Op. 1, No. 10 57

Rode, Pierre (1774–1730)
Etude, No. 3 85
Etude, No. 8 68
Etude, No. 17 13
Etude, No. 18 48

Saint-Saëns, Camille (1835–1921)
Concerto in B Minor, Op. 61 (2nd Movement) 80
Concertstücke, Op. 20 44
Introduction and Rondo Capriccioso, Op. 28 20

Sarasate, Pablo de (1844–1908)
Zigeunerweisen, Op. 20 43

Tchaikovsky, Peter Ilyich (1840–1893)
Concerto in D Major, Op. 35 (1st Movement) 10

Vivaldi, Antonio (1678–1741)
Concerto in D Minor for Two Violins, Op. 3, No. 11 (3rd Movement) ...70

Wieniawski, Henri (1835–1880)
Concerto in D Minor, Op. 22 (2nd Movement) 83
Scherzo Tarantelle, Op. 6 44